Guess What

Published in the United States of America by
Cherry Lake Publishing
Ann Arbor, Michigan
www.cherrylakepublishing.com

Content Adviser: Susan Heinrichs Gray
Reading Adviser: Marla Conn, ReadAbility, Inc.
Book Design: Felicia Macheske

Library of Congress Cataloging-in-Publication Data

Calhoun, Kelly, author.
 Fast and flightless / Kelly Calhoun.
 pages cm. — (Guess what)
 Summary: "Young children are natural problem solvers and always looking for answers, especially when it involves animals. Guess What: Fast and Flightless: Ostrich provides young curious readers with striking visual clues and simply written hints. Using the photos and text, readers rely on visual literacy skills, reading, and reasoning as they solve the animal mystery. Clearly written facts give readers a deeper understanding of how the animal lives. Additional text features, including a glossary and an index, help students locate information and learn new words."— Provided by publisher.
 Audience: Ages 5-8.
 Audience: K to grade 3.
 Includes index.
 ISBN 978-1-63362-627-0 (hardcover) — ISBN 978-1-63362-717-8 (pbk.) — ISBN 978-1-63362-807-6 (pdf) —
 ISBN 978-1-63362-897-7 (ebook)
 1. Ostriches—Juvenile literature. 2. Children's questions and answers. I. Title.

QL696.S9C35 2016
598.5'24—dc23

2015003090

Cherry Lake Publishing would like to acknowledge the work of The Partnership for 21st Century Skills.
Please visit *www.p21.org* for more information.

Printed in the United States of America
Corporate Graphics Inc.

Table of Contents

I have really big eyes.

I have very strong legs and I can run fast.

My body is covered with soft feathers.

I have
a long
neck.

I can
be very
noisy.

13

I have two **toes** and **sharp claws** on my feet.

I have wings, but I cannot fly.

I lay really big eggs.

Do you know what I am?

I'm an Ostrich!

About Ostriches

1. Ostriches can run up to 43 miles per hour.

2. An ostrich can weigh over 300 pounds.

3. Ostriches lay the **largest** eggs of any birds.

4. Ostriches have the largest eyes of any land animal.

5. Ostriches don't need to drink much water in the **desert**.

Glossary

claws (klawz) sharp nails on the foot of an animal

covered (KUHV-urd) with something on top of or in front of it

desert (DEZ-urt) a dry area where hardly any plants grow because there is so little rain

largest (LAHRJ-ist) biggest

noisy (NOI-zee) loud

Index